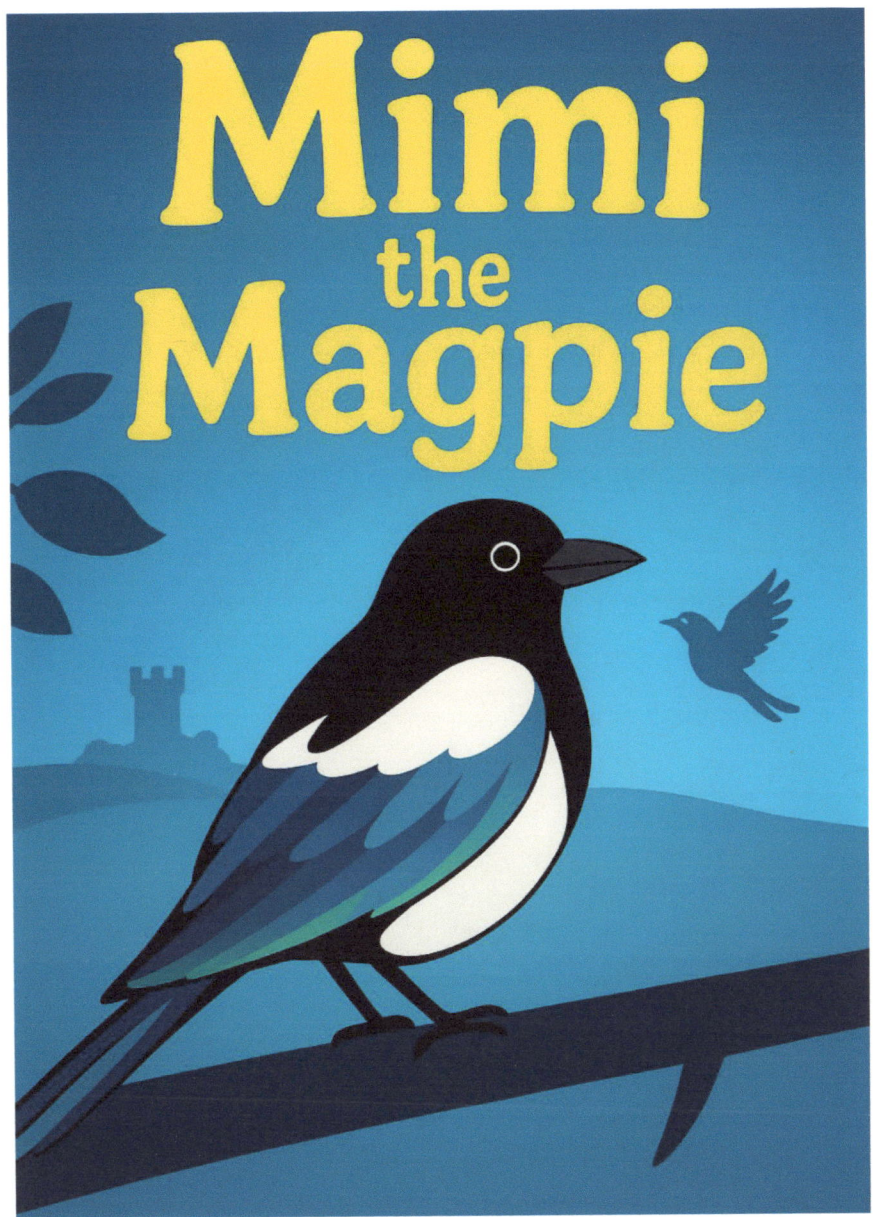

Copyright © 2025 by
Charlie Parrett

ALL RIGHTS RESERVED.

NO part of this book may be reproduced or transmitted in any form by any means, electronic or mechanical, including photocopying and recording, or by any information storage and retrieval system, except as may be expressly permitted in writing from the author.

ISBN:

Dedication

To all those who feel different to others around you, remember you are braver than you believe, stronger than you seem and smarter than you think. (A. A Milne)

Acknowledgment

A special thanks to Authors Solution for believing in this story and making the book come to life.

Mimi the Beautiful Magpie

Mimi the magpie was a little bird with shiny black feathers and bright white wings. When the sunlight danced on her back, it shimmered like diamonds in the sky. Her eyes sparkled with kindness, and she had the sweetest little smile.

Mimi didn't speak like the other magpies, but she had her own kind of magic. She could sort socks by color, make the best feather straw and twig nests, and find quiet ways to show she cared.

Even without saying a word, Mimi was full of beauty and wonder.

The Woodland Chatter

Mimi had a brother who lived high up in the treetop. Every morning, he would call to their mum:

"Chak-chak-chak! Wock-a-wock wock!"

But Mimi never made those sounds. She never had, not since she was a baby magpie. The noise of all the magpie chatter felt too loud for her small ears.

So, whenever the flock started talking chattering too much, Mimi gently covered her ears with her wings and waited quietly for the world to calm down.

A Little Different at School

At magpie school, the other birds noticed Mimi was a bit different. Sometimes, she flapped her wings quickly or rocked back and forth on twig seat.

"Why does she do that?" some magpies whispered.

Millie and Matt, her best friends, understood what others didn't. "Mimi does that when she feels anxious," they would explain. "Sometimes her heart beats so fast it feels like it might burst, and she gets hot and sweaty. It's scary for her." They never laughed or judged, they just cared, and that made all the difference.

The Language of Wings

One afternoon, a new magpie named Juno fluttered over, her eyes bright with kindness.

"Mimi," she chirped sweetly, "I noticed you don't chatter. Do you want to? Maybe I can help?"

Mimi looked away and gave a small shrug of her wings. She didn't like to be in the spotlight, but she wasn't upset. Juno was gentle and just wanted to understand.

Mimi didn't need words to speak. She pointed with her wings, made funny faces, and used *Bird Sign Language*, a clever way to talk using wing shapes and body signs.

Matt, Millie, and now Juno understood her just fine. Even without "chak-chak-chak," Mimi's world was full of conversation.

Mimi's Sock Collection

When she wasn't at school, Mimi had a very important job: *finding socks!*

She found socks on clotheslines, behind the tree stump, near the pond, even in the laundry basket outside the squirrel's house.

She sorted them into piles: short socks, long socks, stripy ones, fluffy ones, and any with holes? Those went straight out!

Sorting socks made her feel calm and happy. The collection grew so big it filled up the whole nest, but Mum just chuckled and let her be.

Mum's Gentle Hope

Mimi's mum sometimes watched her quietly. She hoped, just maybe, one day Mimi would chak like the others. But she never rushed her, never pushed.

Because no matter what, she loved Mimi exactly the way she was, sock collections and all. To her, Mimi's quiet ways and big heart were more magical than any chatter ever could be.

A Sad Feather Day

One day, Mimi's wings drooped and her eyes lost their sparkle.

"Why do you look sad, Mimi?" Mum asked, signing a little frown.

Mimi signed different. Mum hugged her gently, Mimi fluttered, but didn't pull away.

That's when she saw it: under Mum's wing, rainbow feathers! Red, blue, yellow, and green.

Mesmerized, Mimi touched them. They were real.

"See, I'm different too," Mum smiled.

Mimi's heart felt lighter. Maybe she didn't need to change, maybe she just didn't want to feel alone.

The Magic Sock Adventure

Not long after, a wise old squirrel visited Mimi's mum. He wore a leafy cloak and carried a twig walking stick.

He smiled at the socks in the nest. "That little one," he said, "has the heart of a collector and the eyes of a dreamer."

Then, he shared a secret: deep in the woodlands was a glowing magic sock.

"It doesn't change you," he said, "but helps you discover who you truly are."

He then pulled out a tiny, rolled-up scroll, and gave a map that could guide her to the golden sock.

Excited, Mimi fluttered her wings. Maybe the sock wouldn't fix her, but it could help her understand herself.

With Matt and Millie by her side, Mimi set off, curious and proud to be exactly who she was.

Mimi, Matt, and Millie flew toward the woodland. It was not far, just a mile from their nest.

They flew over tall trees with green, dancing leaves. The sky was clear, and a gentle wind helped them along.

Mimi felt happy. She believed that, with her friends, she could find the golden sock.

As they flew, the sun started to go down. The sky turned soft orange, then purple.

"It's getting dark," said Millie.

Mimi pointed with her wing. "Look! We're here!"

They gently landed at the edge of the quiet woodland.

Mimi's Treehouse Camp

"I think we should sleep in the tree above," Mimi said softly. It was their first night away from home, and she felt a little nervous.

Matt and Millie nodded. "Good idea," said Matt.

They decided to work together.

"I'll find sticks to build the base of our camp," said Mimi.

"I'll look for thread to tie the sticks," said Matt.

"And I'll get soft leaves to make our bed," added Millie with a smile.

Soon, they got to work, building their cozy little camp in the tree.

It was morning, and the chirping of birds woke them up. Sunlight peeked through the leaves, making their camp glow, warm and golden.

For breakfast, they each had a sandwich that Mimi's mum had packed. They were soft, tasty, and filled with yummy seeds and berries. Everyone ate until their tummies were full.

After the last bite, Mimi reached into her bag and pulled out the little map.

"Now," she said with a smile, "we go to meet Blaze the Bullfrog!"

The Woodland Pond

Mimi, Matt, and Millie flew off again, the map held tight in Mimi's claws. They were heading to a pond in the middle of the woodland, where Blaze the Bullfrog lived.

Along the way, they passed over thick, dense forests. The trees below looked like a giant green carpet. Suddenly, they spotted something surprising, a circle of mushrooms glowing faintly in the shadows. Tiny fireflies danced above them, forming little patterns in the air.

"Wow!" Millie whispered. "It's like magic lives here."

They flew on, hearts full of wonder, until at last they saw it, the pond. It was wide and still, with dark, murky water that swirled slowly. Matt and Millie landed beside it and looked around. Their eyes widened.

"It doesn't look very clean," Matt said, wrinkling his beak.

"How do we get across the pond?" Mimi asked.

Millie was still staring, wide-eyed at the huge, muddy water.

"It stinks," Mimi sighed.

The smell of the still, dirty water was strong, like old leaves and mud. The only sounds were the frogs going "*croak, croak*" and the crickets singing "*chirp, chirp.*"

"How are we going to get across?" Mimi repeated, frowning.

They all looked around, hoping to find something to help. Then Matt pointed. "Look!" he shouted.

In the greenery, they spotted a small wooden boat, made from twigs and tied together with vines. They climbed in carefully, one by one.

"Let's paddle," said Millie.

And with a gentle push, they began to float across the pond.

Meeting Blaze, The Bullfrog

As they crossed the pond, a dense forest stood ahead. Mimi took out her map and looked closely. "We're almost there," she said with a smile. She fluttered into the forest, and the others followed close behind. The trees were thick, and the sunlight barely touched the ground. After a while, they came out into the light, and there, sitting on a giant leaf, was Blaze the Bullfrog!

"Blaze!" Mimi called.

He gave a slow, happy blink. "Welcome, travelers," he said.

"We're looking for the golden sock," Matt said.

"You're very close," Blaze replied. "To the east, there's a big tree full of fruits. Look carefully, it has a golden sock hanging from one of its branches."

The three friends cheered. "Thank you, Blaze!" they said together. Then they turned and headed east, hope fluttering in their hearts.

The Sock, And The Spark Inside

After flying for just a few minutes, Mimi saw it, a big tree standing tall and proud.

"There it is!" Mimi shouted with excitement.

Matt and Millie looked where she was pointing. The tree was full of bright, colourful fruits and covered in birds of all kinds. The branches swayed gently as the birds chirped and sang, as if they were welcoming Mimi and her friends.

And there it was. *The Magic Sock.* It hung from a golden branch, glittering softly in the woodland light. Mimi stepped forward slowly. She looked at it closely, her heart full of wonder.

She thought of her rocking, her flapping, her rainbow-feathered mum, and how she always taught Mimi to be kind and helpful to everyone, because that was the real spark of a good heart.

And slowly… Mimi stepped back.

The lessons from her mum danced in her heart. They had shown her that magic wasn't in the sock, it was already inside her. She smiled.

"I don't need the sock," she signed. "I like being me."

Fun Activities

- **Design a Magic Sock:** Use crayons, glitter, or stickers to make your own sock that shows what makes YOU special!

- **Learn Bird Sign Language:** Try fun signs like "happy," "friend," and "hello" using your arms and hands!

- **Silly Sock Sort:** Bring in socks from home and sort them like Mimi, by color, length, or fluffiness!

- **Rainbow Feathers Craft:** Color your own magpie with a rainbow wing to celebrate what makes you *different and dazzling!*

- **Difference Tree:** Create a tree where children can add leaves with words or drawings representing their unique traits.

Author's Bio

Charlie lives in the beautiful city of Worcester. She graduated with a BSc Hons Psychology and is currently completing an online Higher Access course in Medical and Health Science. She enjoys furthering her academic qualifications as well as spending time with her family and her gorgeous flat-coated retriever, Zazie, who brings her much joy and socks and sticks too! Charlie is part of the LGBTQ community and her journey has influenced her writing, in that she hopes her writing will resonate with others.

www.ingramcontent.com/pod-product-compliance
Lightning Source LLC
Chambersburg PA
CBHW040300100526
44584CB00004BA/289